MAKING A TAVERN TABLE

JIM RENDI

Schiffer Publishing Ltd

4880 Lower Valley Road, Atglen, PA 19310 USA

Contents

Library of Congress Card Number: 2002109102

Designed by Kevin Kelly
Cover by Bruce Waters
Type set in Americana BT/Korinna BT

ISBN: 0-7643-1677-X
Printed in China

Published by Schiffer Publishing Ltd.
4880 Lower Valley Road
Atglen, PA 19310
Phone: (610) 593-1777; Fax: (610) 593-2002
E-mail: Schifferbk@aol.com
Please visit our web site catalog at **www.schifferbooks.com**
We are always looking for people to write books on new and related subjects. If you have an idea for a book please contact us at the above address.

This book may be purchased from the publisher.
Include $3.95 for shipping.
Please try your bookstore first.
You may write for a free catalog.

In Europe, Schiffer books are distributed by
Bushwood Books
6 Marksbury Ave.
Kew Gardens
Surrey TW9 4JF England
Phone: 44 (0) 20 8392-8585; Fax: 44 (0) 20 8392-9876
E-mail: Bushwd@aol.com
Free postage in the U.K., Europe; air mail at cost.

Introduction

Several years ago I published a book on building a Windsor chair. Even then the thought was that I would make an accompanying book on tavern tables. They just seem to go together! Well, it took longer than I expected for a variety of reasons, one of which was that the first book created many demands on my time. But here it is.

The tavern table design originated in the earlier colonial period of the 17th and 18th century. It gets its name from the fact the tables in that early taverns were often of this construction. Considered a stretcher base table, it was built for its utility and its structural strength. This becomes obvious when this table is compared with its contemporary Queen Anne style table, which had cabriole legs and no stretchers. Relatively simply to make, the mortise and tenon frame with aprons and stretchers provided a solid, graceful form, easily produced by the local craftsman.

The most decorative aspect to the table is the leg, and it becomes the focal point. Many options can be explored for the leg. Books about early furniture have many examples, and Wallace Nutting's classic *Furniture Treasury* offers some drawings that may get your creative juices flowing. See especially plates 4680-86.

The name should not limit our understanding of the table. This same form found its way into the home and businesses of early America. In the great room/kitchen it was often the central working/eating area for the colonial family. In early business it proudly displayed the goods that were offered for sale. Beyond that, its basic structure in a variety of styles served for everything from footstools to smoking tables.

This versatility and simple elegance still serves us well today. A large table, like the one shown in this project, could well serve as a dining room table, surrounded by graceful Windsor chairs. A little longer with, perhaps a double base, and it is the perfect table for a boardroom. Shorter and smaller it is a great coffee table. And in with a drawer or two it might be a great computer table.

In short, the design of this table is timeless. I hope you enjoy building it and using it for many years to come.

Bill of Materials

For an 84" x 40" x 30" tavern table you will need the following wood. Smaller tables may also be made using these methods, with corresponding adjustment to the wood.

Tabletop:	Supplies of 5/4 rough lumber sufficient to create a finished top that measures 84" x 40" x 1".
Legs:	4 @ 3" x 3" x 30"
Aprons:	2 @ 6" x 1" x 27-1/8"
	2 @ 6" x 1" x 60"
Stretchers	2 @ 1" x 3-3/4" x 27"
	1 @ 1" x 3-3/4" x 60"
Pins	4 @ 2-1/2" x 2-1/2" x 6"

The Drawings

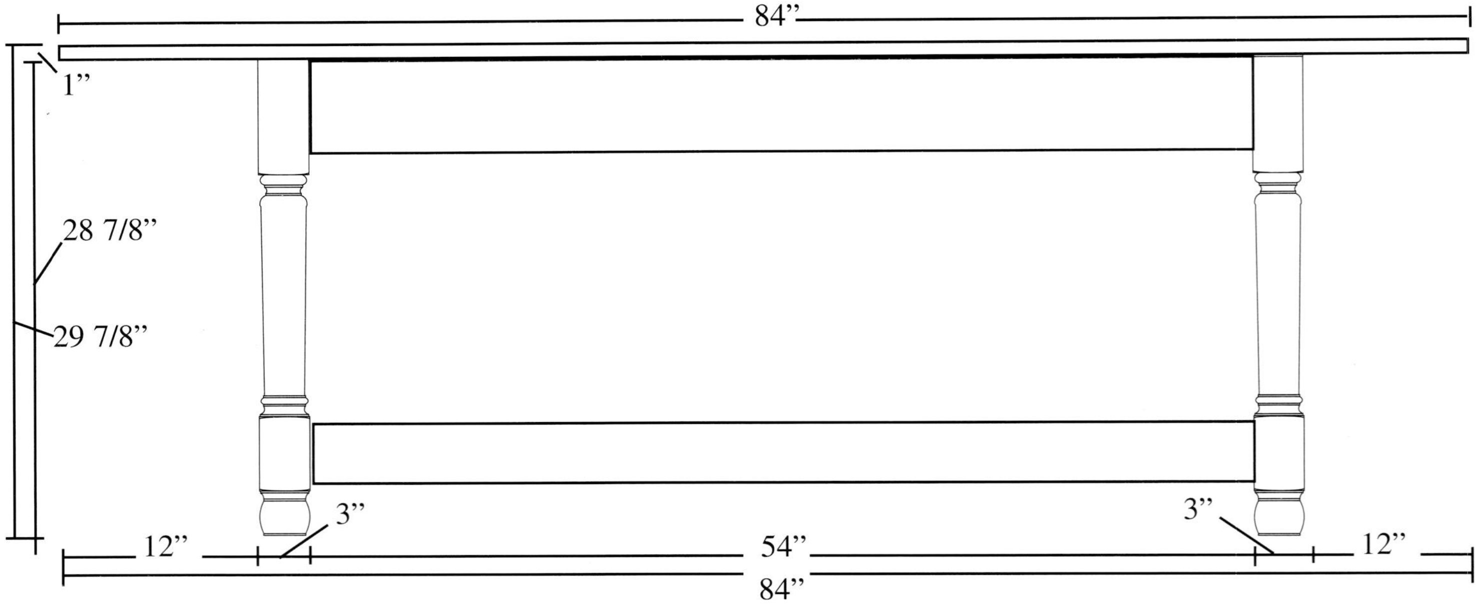

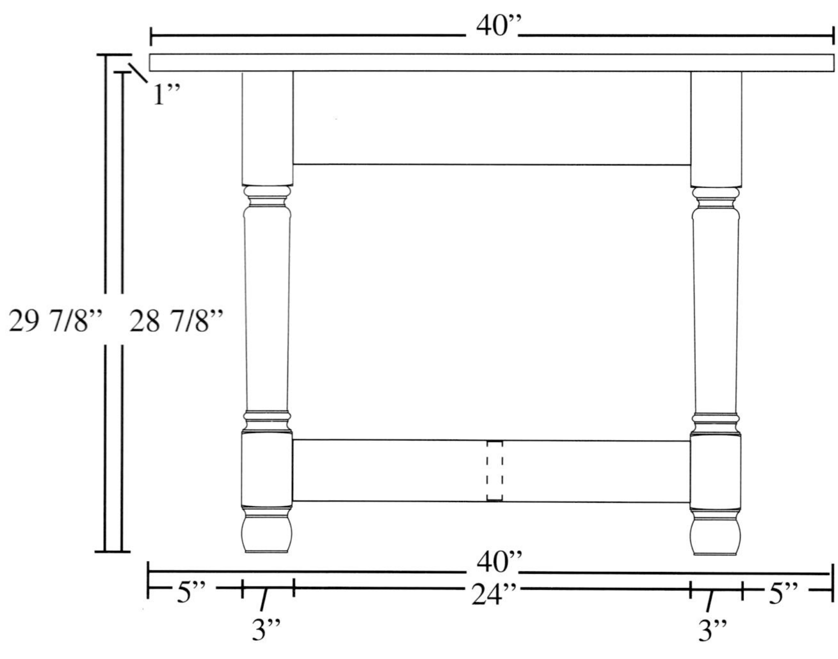

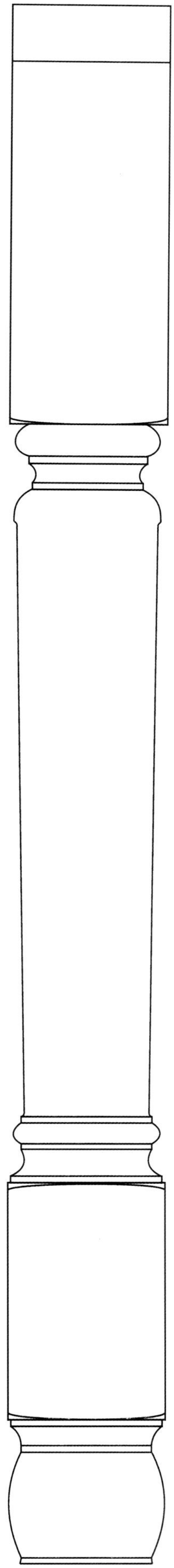

Excess: 1-1/8"
Apron
Block: 7"
Align pattern here
Bead: 5/8"
Fillet: 1/8"
Cove: 3/8"
Fillet: 1/8"
Half bead: 5/8"

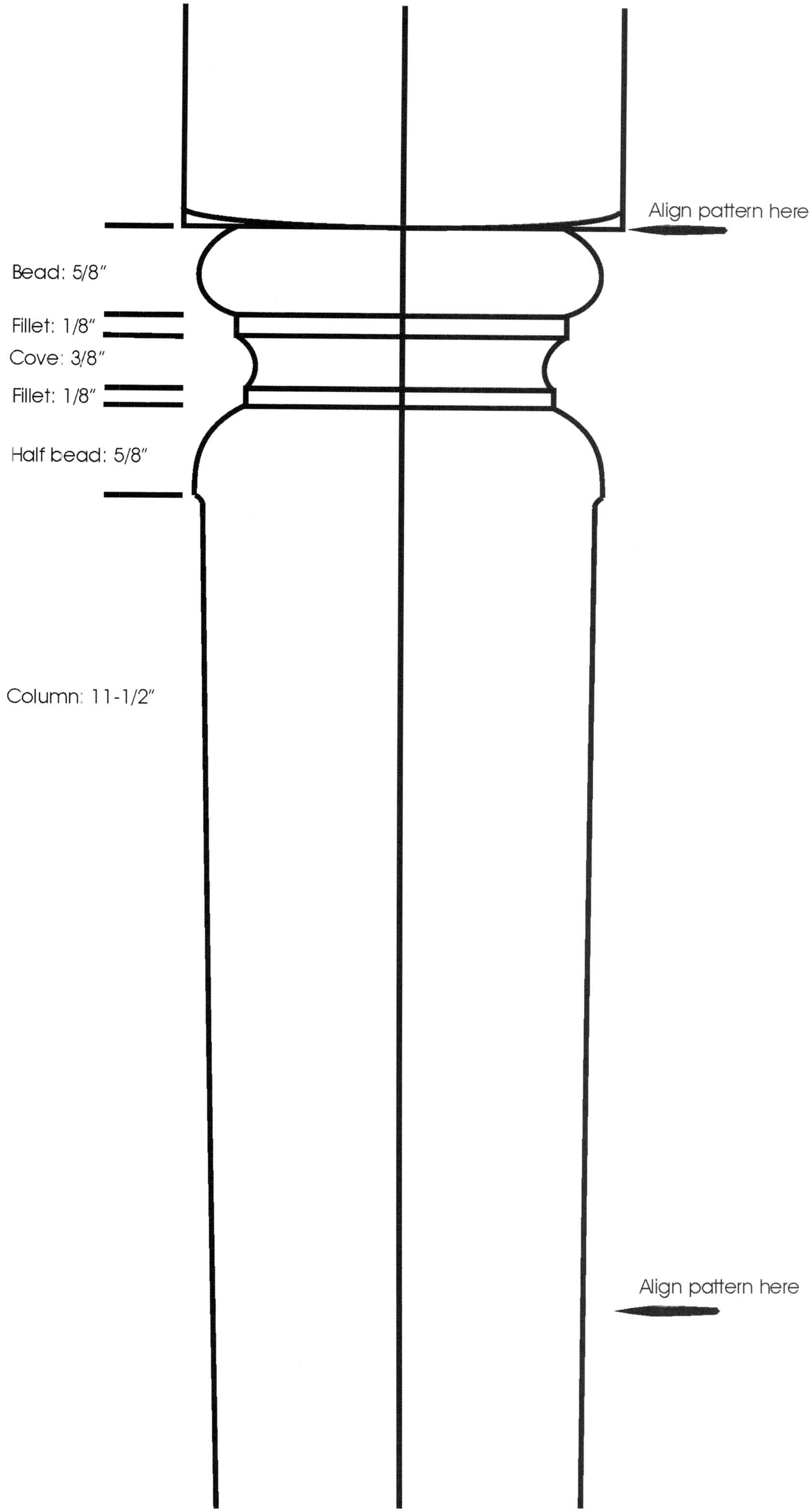
Align pattern here
Bead: 5/8″
Fillet: 1/8″
Cove: 3/8″
Fillet: 1/8″
Half bead: 5/8″
Column: 11-1/2″
Align pattern here

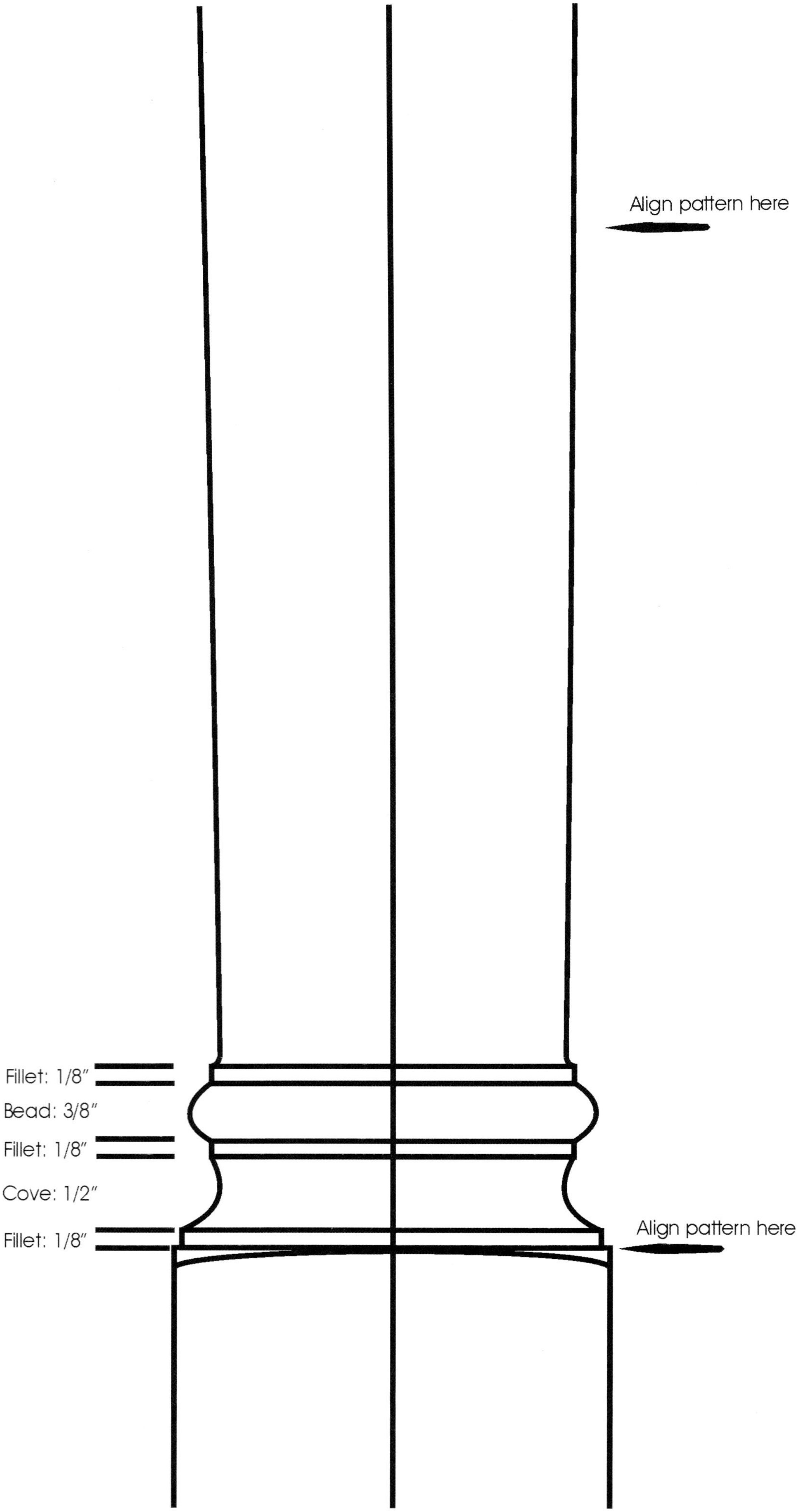

Align pattern here
Fillet: 1/8″
Bead: 3/8″
Fillet: 1/8″
Cove: 1/2″
Fillet: 1/8″
Align pattern here

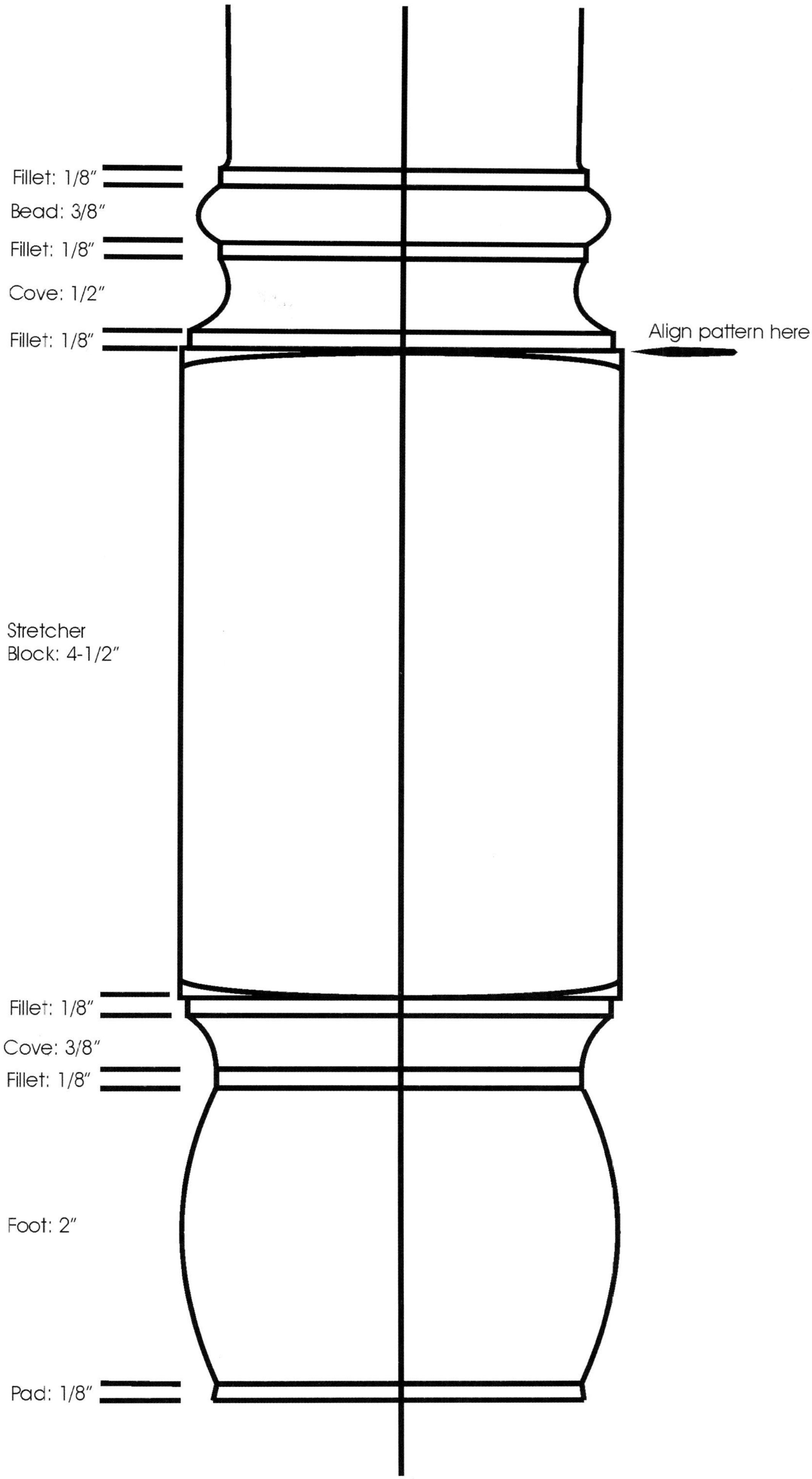
Fillet: 1/8″
Bead: 3/8″
Fillet: 1/8″
Cove: 1/2″
Fillet: 1/8″
Align pattern here
Stretcher
Block: 4-1/2″
Fillet: 1/8″
Cove: 3/8″
Fillet: 1/8″
Foot: 2″
Pad: 1/8″

The Tabletop

The table top for the project is 84" x by 40" x 1". It is made up of a number of narrower planks, joined and glued together. Even though the boards were planed and ripped roughly to size mechanically, they need some finishing touches with a plane to insure a proper joint.

We will be planing along an 84" edge, which means we need a reliable holding mechanism. The simplest is two boards clamped to the work table angled slightly toward each other. The board to be planed is held in place where the boards narrow, and planing is done in that direction.

It is important to hold the plane properly to keep it flat during the shaving. The thumb of the left hand should rest above the plate, with the fingers running along the side of the board. The right hand holds the handle with the forefinger riding along the side of the blade to control and position the plane.

We have a surface-planed board that has been rip-sawn at the mill. While fairly smooth, the saw cut does not give the best joint. Saws leave marks and are not always even. To fix this, we use a hand plane. Walk with the plane, applying pressure with your right hand behind the blade and downward pressure with your left hand. At the end of the stroke, do not drag the plane back across the surface; the friction will dull the blade.

A number seven or eight Stanley joiner plane, with its long sole, is designed for a job like this.

Use a square to be sure the planed surface is perpendicular to the to the adjoining surfaces. Check along the length of the board.

To check the joint, place one planed surface on top of the other. I like to step it back just slightly, because I find it easier to spot problems this way.

Another indication of squareness is that you get a continuous shave through the length of the board. You must, of course, have sharp tools for this.

Because of the variations in pressure while hand planing you get some high and low crowns. I have a slight one here. Maintaining even pressure through the length of the shave will help to ensure a straight line.

This "d" with an arrow marks the face of the board and points to the edge to be joined. Mark the face and edge of the other piece to be joined. Repeat the planing process on the second board.

Plane to remove the crown. Start with light pressure, increase pressure over the crown and reduce pressure as you end the cut. Remember this follow-through process; it is a basic procedure in woodworking.

Recheck the alignment and make further adjustments. Note plane in the foreground. I don't rest a plane on its blade or side to protect against damage. In this case the blade is held up by the shavings beneath the footplate.

Another way is to align the boards edge to edge and hold a straight edge against the surfaces. At the top everything looks perfect, but at the bottom, the gap shows the edge to be cut on an angle.

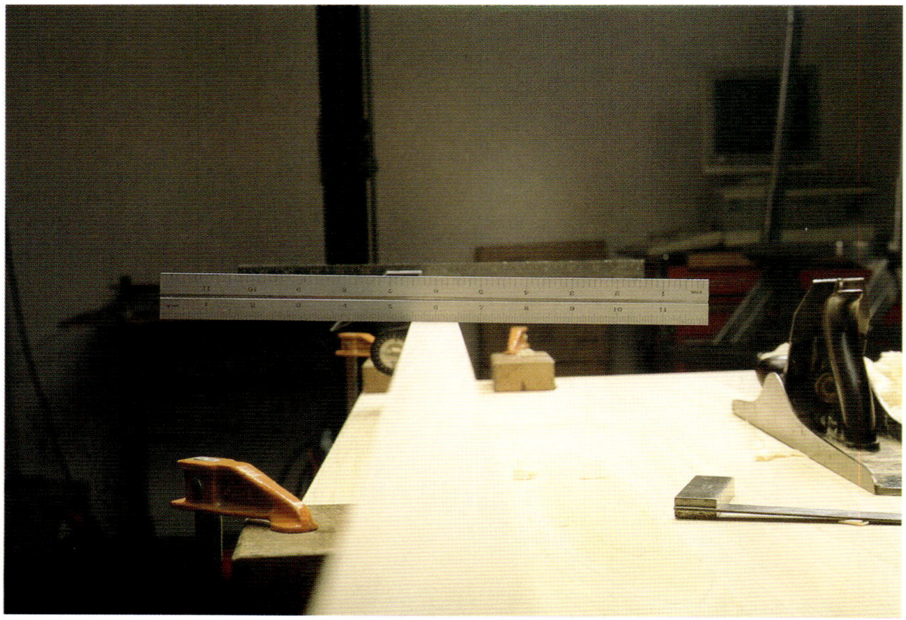

Resting two-story sticks and eyeballing them can show if the cut is perfectly even. In this case the two sticks are simply metal rulers with straight edges balanced on the planed edge. If you compare them you will see that they are not parallel, which indicates that the joint surface is not flat.

To adjust for a high side, first check that your plane blade is square across its mouth. Then make another shave, applying more pressure to the high side. Check after each shave to see your progress. This is a difficult process and requires attention to detail. You may want to practice on shorter lengths and progress to longer boards, if you are designing a table to the book's length.

Adjust the blade depth and mouth to get the finest shaving you can.

Winding sticks are simply two sticks of equal thickness. Plane two pieces together for an exact match.

Make the edge of one stick black.

Rest the sticks on the edge of the board. When sighting down the board the edges of the sticks should be parallel. You can see that here they are not in alignment.

After adjustment the sticks align well. Make a final check along the length of the board. Put one stick at the far end, and move the second to various positions along the length.

Carefully glue and clamp the boards together. Use a brace to keep them flat and clean any excess glue before it dries.

After adjustment the boards are perfectly straight, and ready to be glued.

After the glue has dried and the clamps are removed, there are some things that need to be done to the joined top. First remove excess glue from the joints. I am using a roughing chisel, but a paint scraper could be used as well. Taking away the glue prevents the blade of the plane from being nicked in future steps.

Make a triangular mark to show where the boards are meant to go together. Continue with the process with the other boards to be joined to form the tabletop. When all the pieces are joined, align them using the triangles, glue all edges, and clamp them top together.

To smooth the surface of the tabletop I use a fore or trying plane, with a blade that has been crowned to act as a roughing plane. Slicing across the grain at an angle levels the surface.

Final preparation is done with scraper.

After using the curved plane, use the joiner plane going with the grain to smooth any planing marks.

Any marks can be sanded away.

Next the joiner plane marks are smoothed by the smoothing plane. The blade's corner edges are slightly rounded to prevent shaving lines from developing. No matter, on soft woods like poplar or pine you can sand them out. On harder woods, like maple or birch, you can use a cabinet scraper.

Building the Base

We begin the base by choosing the design for the legs. In the simple structure of the tavern table the legs are the most decorative element and allow for some of the table maker's creativity to show through. Here you see three early tavern table leg patterns, reminiscent of the 18th century. Two of them are shown with their story sticks, marked with the profile of the pattern.

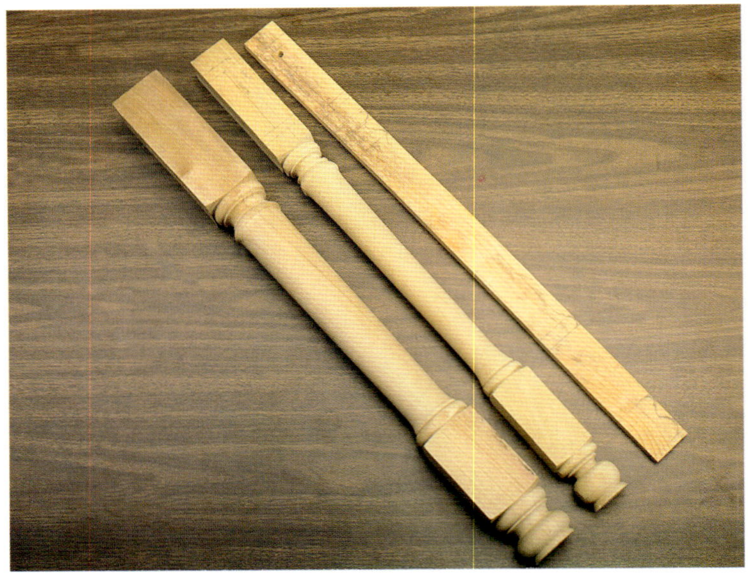

Here you see the same design used with different sizes of stock. The results are quite different. For the tavern table I like the thicker version.

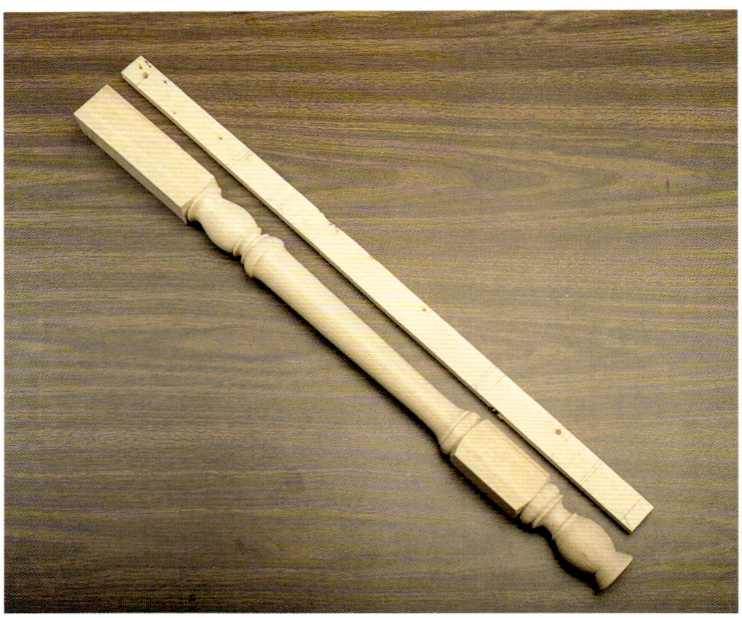

This leg design came from an early Queen Anne chest-on-frame.

Looked at the over all design. The foot here is a little diminutive for the large table we are making. It is a good idea to turn several possible designs in scrap wood until you get the one you like.

My next design experiment generated the foot on the right. This also seemed a little too small, and I reacted negatively to it, but uou may like it. The variations are endless, yet historically some designs were repeated more often.

There are two block sections, one near the bottom for stretchers and one at the top for the apron. The bottom block is 4-1/2" long.

The design I ended with is on the right of this photograph. It has the bulk and aesthetics I like. Of course everyone approaches the work with a different sensibility, and each maker will create a piece that is uniquely his or her own, based on their own vision of what is beautiful. You are in control of the final product.

The top block is 7" long to accommodate the apron.

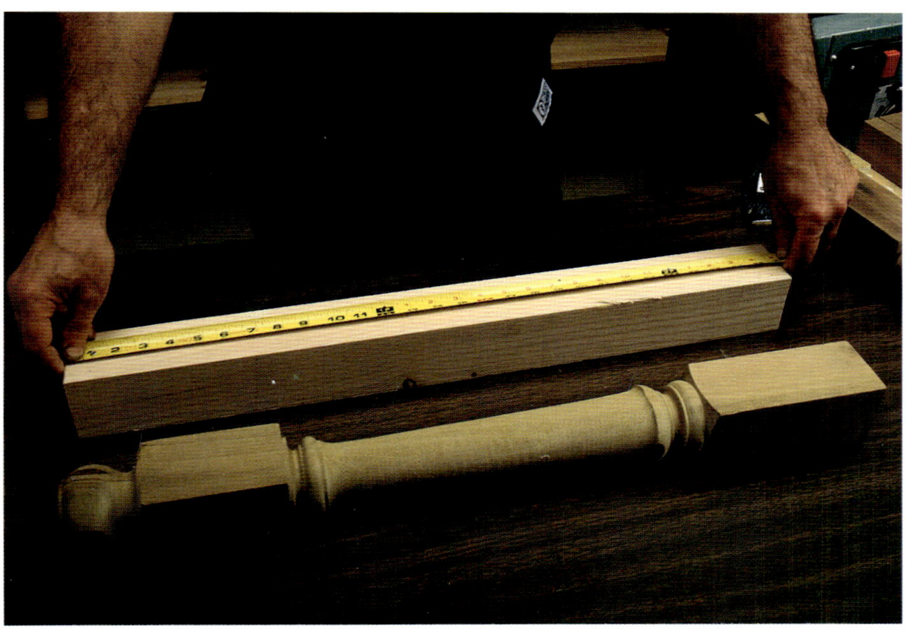

Now that I have a foot design I like, I need to lay out the rest of the leg. This is a large table, 84 inches by 40 inches, so I need a heavy leg. I will work with 3" x 3" x 30" stock.

Begin to mark the blank at the foot. It is 2-3/4" from the bottom.

Above it is the 4-1/2" bottom block.

This is followed a 1/8" fillet, followed by a 1/2" cove section with a 1/8" fillet above it.

These are followed by a bead that is 3/8".

Above this is another 1/8" fillet.

The column is next. It is about 11-1/2" measuring 20" **from the bottom of the foot.**

At the top o the column is a half bead, 5/8".

Above the half bead is a 1/8" fillet

a 3/8" cove...

another 1/8" fillet...

and a 5/8" bead. 1" above the bead mark the bottom of the apron and 1/2" above that mark the bottom of the mortise.

The ends of blocks get a slight shaping, about 1/8". I usually just make this cut by eye during the turning.

Put the blanks for the four legs side by side and draw the guidelines for the segments.

Finally, we mark the foot. Working down from the top of the foot draw lines for a 1/8" fillet, a 1/2" cove, and a 1/8" fillet.

Measure up 1" from the top of the uppermost foot fillet and mark. This is the bottom of the stretcher.

Measure up another 1/2" and mark the bottom of the mortise.

Measure up from the bottom of the apron 6", the height of the apron. (Notice that this does not go to the top of the wood.)

This top 1-1/8" is extra, left here until after the turning and mortising for added strength.

This is a rosewood mortising marking gauge. Two spikes mark the width of the mortise.

Measure down 5/8" from the top of the apron. This is will allow for the haunch at the top of the tenon and matches the width of the mortise.

The width is adjusted by a turn screw at the end of the handle.

To set the position of the mortise, find the center of the block...

Set the marking gauge to the width of the mortise by laying the mortising chisel between the spikes and adjusting them until they touch each side of the chisel.

and measure half the width of the mortise on each side of it. In this case that is 5/16".

Line up the spikes of the marker and set the position. You can check this for center by moving the gauge to the other side of the block and making sure the marks match.

Mark the lines all the way through the apron block portion of the leg. Do this on two adjoining sides.

Continue the lines around the end so they meet in the center.

The result. These end lines determine the depth of the mortise.

Set a single marking gauge to the thickness of the mortise and mark the ends of the block.

For roughing in the mortise, choose a drill bit slightly smaller than your mortise size. In this case we chose a 1/2" Forstner bit. Align the center of the mortise with the bit and set a fence. Set the depth of the hole to 1-5/8".

This will determine the depth of the mortise at the haunch.

Make a hole at one end of the mortise...

When you have done whole length, go back and drill between the holes.

and the other. This sets the boundaries.

Do the adjoining side the same way. This will complete the rough mortises, which we will return to after turning the legs.

Continue along the line between the holes. These holes should be more or less edge to edge.

Mark the center of the ends by drawing lines diagonally.

Set the drive center at the top of the leg. This will keep the head-piece out of the way of the turning.

in both directions. Repeat on the other end.

Place the live center in the bottom and tighten the leg in place.

Be sure to tighten the various holding mechanisms for safety. The tool rest should be parallel to the blank and slightly below center.

Begin working around the block at the bottom of the leg. Use the long point of the skew to establish clean corners of the square section. Begin going straight in at a 90-degree angle.

Then angle your cut slightly to the right to open it up.

Next go slightly to the left.

Repeat at the top of the block. Straight in...

slightly to the right...

slightly to the left.

Repeat the process on the bottom edge of the top block.

At the bottom of the leg, use the parting tool, cutting straight in to create the fillet below...

and above the stretcher block.

Since both of these fillets abut a cove, you can widen your cut in the direction of the cove to give you more access. Do not cut toward the block!

Continue until the fillet is completely round. The finished diameter of the fillets above and below the stretcher block will be 2-7/8"

Set your caliper to the correct diameter and continue with the parting tool until the caliper fits over the turning.

Next we cut the fillet above ball foot. Because the foot rounds down from the fillet and it abuts a cove at the top, you can start with the parting tool instead of the skew.

Cut the fillet down to a diameter of 2-1/2". For convenience you may also remove wood in the direction of the cove above the fillet.

To create more workspace, next I will give the underside of the block its slight (1/8") shaping. Use a skew, holding it perpendicular to the work. With the long point leading, and the angle of the skew slightly tilted, give a sweeping curve to the surface.

Use a gouge to take the foot section down to round.

The result.

A gentle touch will reveal flat spots that the eye may miss. I emphasize gentle to avoid injury. If you are unsure, simply turn off the lathe and examine the turning.

Between the two fillets create a cove, using a gouge. This is an asymmetrical cove, moving between the 2-7/8" upper fillet and the 2-1/2" lower fillet. Use your drawing and your eye to arrive at a pleasing curve.

Continue round the whole foot.

Next I round the foot. I begin three quarters of the way up and work toward the fillet.

The pad is created by leaving space at the end of this curve.

Next I start one quarter of the way up and work toward the pad.

Bevel the edge of the pad holding the parting tool at a slight angle.

Also create a slight bevel to the fillet above the foot, using a skew.

Continue with the parting tool and smooth the bottom surface. Work in from the circumference. This will insure a flat bottom.

When the pad and fillet are defined, use a gouge to finish off the ball.

If a gouge seems difficult to use for creating the cove, an alternative is a scraping tool.

Another alternative. When creating bevels, use the long point of a skew.

Two incised lines, above and below center, add a decorative touch.

Next we move above the stretcher block. We have already set a fillet above the block. Above this is a cove, followed by 2-1/2" diameter fillet, a bead, and another 2-1/2" fillet. Begin by shaping the upper surface of the block. Again, this opens up the workspace.

Begin the fillets to define their position, but do not take them to their final diameter.

Progress.

Reduce the lower section of the column to round, making it easier to work.

Now reduce the fillets to their 2-1/2" diameter.

Rough in the cove to define the area.

Rough down the column and the bead to give more workspace.

Take the bead area down to a diameter of 2-3/4".

With the bead diameter established reduce the lower column. The diameter at the bottom is less than the fillet, so you can use the fillet as a visual guide.

Creating a bead is the most difficult part of turning. Working from the center out use a 1/4" ladyfinger gouge to roll the bead. This is one of the easiest tools to use to accomplish this task. Small beads can be worked with a skew or a parting tool also.

Make a couple of passes with the tool.

Use the same tool to finish the cove. With the cove, work toward the center, ending up with the curve of the blade at a slight angle at the center.

Alternatively, a scraping tool may be used.

Now we move to the top of the column. If you have trouble seeing the guidelines as the piece turns, continue them onto a second side. This should make them more visible on the spinning piece.

Use a parting tool to clean up the top surface of the block and put a slight bevel to the fillet.

Before turning, it is a good idea to refresh your memory about the design elements. Return to the pattern and mark the various features.

Progress

First we want to define the bottom edge of the apron block. Begin with a skew. This is less likely to tear the work on the initial cut. Hold the tool perpendicular to the turning, and lift the handle to move the blade into the work.

Reduce the upper column until the lines almost disappear. Leave a trace of the line to define the areas.

After the initial cut, angle the skew left…

Beneath the block use the parting tool to bring the wood to round.

and right to open up the cut. Repeat this several times.

Define the two fillet areas. The larger one, just below the bead is 2-1/4". The smaller one, just above the half bead, is 2-1/8".

Now bring the whole upper section, below the apron block to round. Redraw any lines you erase.

Roughly reduce the cove between the fillets, to get it out of the way and help define the areas.

Bevel the bottom surface of the block. This allows better access for creating the top of the bead.

Use the long point of the skew to define the upper shoulder of the bead.

Continue with the gouge to shape the cove.

Switch to the ladyfinger 1/4" gouge to shape the bottom of the bead.

Use the large roughing gouge to give shape to the taper of the column.

The result is a roughed out shape, between the fillet at the bottom of the column and the half bead at the top.

Define the half bead by rolling the gouge.

The same kind of sweep is at the bottom, coming out to the fillet that is there.

Use a large gouge to finish up the column. Start at the top, under the half bead. The column ends in a small sweep then comes out to the edge of the half bead.

When the sweeping ends are defined, shape the column to join them.

The basic shape is set.

To clean up the column always go "downhill," moving from a larger section to a smaller section. You can use a gouge held at a 45-degree angle…

or a skew, like this.

To sand the piece, I hold the paper so it is behind and underneath. There is less chance of it catching and causing injury to you or your work.

For finishing the mortises and cutting the tenons, we need the single and double marking gauges, a mortising chisel, a Stanley #90 shoulder plane, a 9-1/4 Stanley block plane, tenon back saws, a wide chisel, a square, and either a wooden mallet or a soft head hammer.

To clean up the mortises, use the widest possible chisel and slice down the side of the mortise. You may need to repeat this several times to get to the final dimension. Do this on both sides, being careful to hold the chisel square to its side.

Use a thinner chisel to square off the ends of the mortise in the same way.

Saw the line of the mortise down to the haunch mark.

Note the line made earlier on the end for the haunch.

Remove the haunch piece in 1/8" to 1/4" slices.

When it is removed, use the chisel to smooth it flat.

The end aprons are 5-3/4" x 1" x 27-1/8" overall. After considering the 1-1/2" tenons, the apron will be 24". Prepare the board and mark the face side and top edge.

Carry the mark all away around.

Mark the 1-1/2" depth of the tenon on each end.

Align the apron with the line marking the top of the leg (remember we still have an extra 1" at the top of the leg for strength). Then mark the top of the mortise...

and the bottom.

Carry the lines around the mortise.

Carefully holding a square along the line of the mortise shoulder, scribe the line using the edge of your chisel. Mark it lightly, being sure to keep the square in place and the chisel flush against it.

Retrace the line with more pressure, and then once without the square in place. When the line is deeply inscribed, slice back to it from the waste side with the chisel to create a half v-line. This will help make an exposed clean shoulder for the joint.

Mark the width of the tenon on the opposite side of the apron.

Mark the waste side with an X.

With a single marking gauge carry this mark down the end of the tenon.

Secure the apron piece with the board tilted forward. Start at the back corner, and begin to cut on the line of the tenon. This position will allow the saw to be horizontal.

Gradually angle the blade down so you are cutting the length of the line.

When the heel of the saw reaches the line, reposition the board so the end is horizontal, and continue down to the line on both sides.

Cut the side of the tenon. Begin at the far side with the blade on the waste side of the mark.

Walk the saw down until you are cutting horizontally.

Mark and saw to the bottom shoulder.

Mark the haunch on the upper shoulder...

and saw down to it.

Finish the haunch cut.

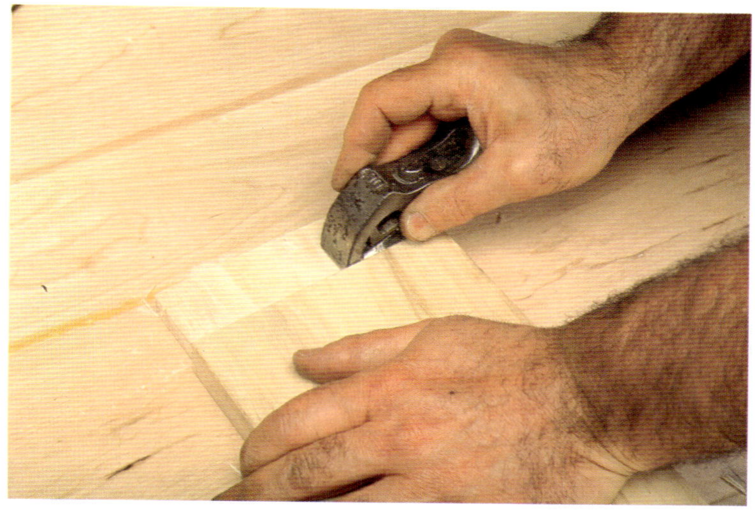

Use the # 90 shoulder plane to trim the tenon.

The result.

Alternatively you can use a wide chisel held flat. Keep adjusting until it fits.

Check the fit. This is a little heavy.

Use the block plane to trim the edges, making for an easier fit.

The tenons of the apron come together in the leg, so it is necessary to bevel the inside corners.

With the four legs lined up, carry the lines to all of the stretcher blocks.

Use the double marking gauge to define the sides of the mortise.

The end stretchers are 1" x 3-3/4" x 27". The stretchers are in an H-pattern with a stretcher connecting the legs at each short end, and a central stretcher running between. Set the four legs in their relative position and mark the correct side for the stretcher. The mortise will be centered on the stretcher block in both directions. It will be 5/8" thick and 3" wide. Mark the edges of the stretcher on the block, and measuring in 3/8" from each edge, mark the width of the tenon.

As before, use a drill press to remove wood from the mortise and clean the cut with chisels.

Mark the face side and the top of the stretcher, then mark the position of the tenon.

Mark the line of the shoulder, 1-1/2" from the end.

Working from the face side use the double marking gauge to define the thickness of the tenon.

Continue around the end and other side. Repeat on each of the end stretchers. Remember the shoulder to shoulder length of the end stretcher is the same as that of the end apron.

Cut down on the tenon as before. This time I start at the front and walk my saw down at the back until I establish a level cut. This is because the board is smaller.

Cut the shoulder starting with the front of the saw with a light touch...

and working the heel of the saw down as the cut is established.

Mark the width of the tenon and cut down to the shoulder.

Cut away the waste at the shoulder.

Clean up the tenon with the plane.

The result.

Test the fit. The tenon should fit snugly in the mortise, but not too tightly. It should be able to be seated using hand pressure alone.

For the side overhangs we will use 5 inches on each side, a figure we arrived at before setting the length of the end stretchers and aprons.

Assemble the end of the undercarriage for a test fit. Do not glue yet. Make the necessary adjustments.

Use these assemblies to help determine the amount of overhang you want. Stand the end assemblies on the table. The overhang is variable depending on your taste and the aesthetics of the piece. This is an 84" table meant for dining, so I want a generous overhang at the ends. In this case I will use twelve inches. Never use more than twenty-four inches.

The rough length of the front and back aprons can be determined by subtracting the two overhangs (24" total) from the length of the tabletop (84"). That means the rough length of the aprons will be 60". The board I will use is in need of some clean-up even though it has been through the joiner. I do the smoothing before cutting tenons. After securing the work to the work area I use a well-tuned Stanley #4 smoothing plane. Hold the plane at an angle and move it straight down the board to make a slicing cut. If your plane is sharp and set correctly, this will give you a surface that is as good or better than a sanded surface.

Alternatively you can use a block plane in the same way. Planing eliminates most of the need for sand paper and its attending noise and dust.

A cabinet scraper like this Stanley #80 makes a nice final step.

Mark the face surface and top edge of the apron. The board is now ready for fitting.

Mark the top of the tenon...

With the surface and top of the apron in the proper position, align the top edge of the apron with the mark for the top on the apron block.

and the bottom of the tenon.

Mark the thickness of the tenon. The shoulder is on the facing surface. This will allow you to set the marking gauge. **Note:** As you mark the tenon make also mark the apron to the leg with matching numbers. This will assure that when they are rejoined later the fit will be correct.

Set the marking gauge from the face side and mark the thickness of the tenon.

Measure the length of the tenon from the end, 1-3/4", and mark the facing surface.

Working from the facing surface use a square to mark the edges.

Continue the mark around to the sides.

Mark the areas to be removed with an X.

Because it is a long board, I need to cut the tenon a little differently. Having rigged my clamps, I start at the near side, go part way, and turn the board around. Finish the cutting of the tenon as you did on the side aprons.

With the tenon seated in the leg...

measure from the outside of the leg 5 feet, to get the overall length of the table base.

Square the mark and lay the outside of the apron block to it. Strike a line on the on the apron, along the inside of the apron block. This will give you the line of the shoulder of the tenon.

Dry clamp the table base together and check all the joints. Take a measure of the outside length (in this table it is 5 feet exactly)...

Measure out from the shoulder line 1-3/4". This will be the end of the tenon, and the apron should be cut off here. Cut the tenon as on the other end.

and the outside width (30")

Finally check the squareness by measuring the diagonals from the outside corners. If they match you are in business. If not, adjust to square by fine tuning with diagonal clamps across the corners.

Lay the board to be used for the center stretcher between the side stretchers. Mark the length. This will give you an accurate measurement for this piece. **Remember that the two 1/2" tenons need to be added to this when laying out the stretcher.**

The top edge of the end stretchers is going to be slightly rounded, so the height of the center stretcher needs to be somewhat less. The side stretchers are 3-3/4" high, so the center stretcher is 3-1/2" high.

Mark the center of the end stretcher.

From the center mark of the end stretcher, mark the thickness of the center stretcher, in this case 1", which is 1/2" on each side of center.

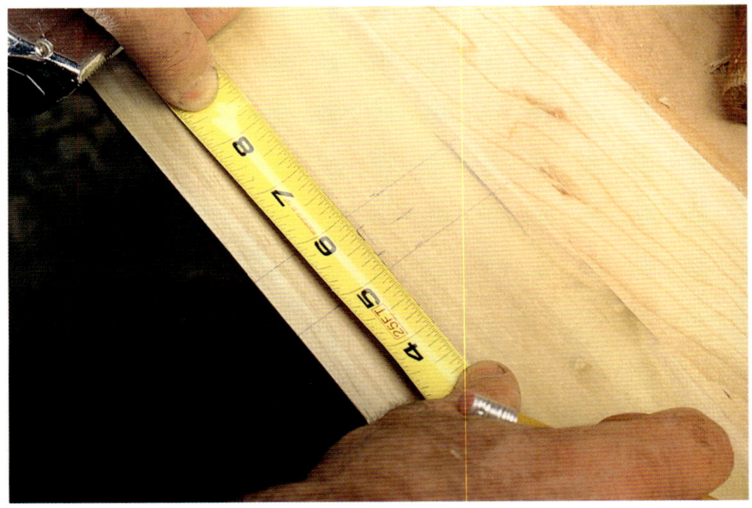

Also from the center of the mortise measure out to accommodate the tenon. We will use a 1/2" thick tenon, so measure out 1/4" from center. This leaves a shoulder of 1/4" on each side.

Square the lines to mark out the thickness of the stretcher.

Mark a top and bottom shoulder of 1/4".

Align the two end stretchers together, top edge touching and inside surface up. Continue the lines from one to the other.

Set the drill depth to 1/2" and drill out the mortises as before.

Clean up the cut with the chisels. Start with corner of the chisel and slice down, gradually turning the chisel to vertical. You are cutting across the grain, which requires a little different technique.

Measure and cut the four-shoulder tenon on one end of the center stretcher. Use the same technique as on the tenons of the end stretchers, though keeping to a 1/2" depth.

Fit the tenon into the mortise at one end. Be sure the bottom is flush with the bottom of the end stretcher, and the joint is tight. If all is well, cut the other tenon.

Now we are ready for some decorative touches. On the bottom edge of the apron I am going to add a quarter edge bead. Double check that you are working on the correct surface and the correct edge. As you are setting up it is a good time to do some clean-ups. If we had done some of this earlier, the chances of marring it would have been much greater.

With this size table I am going to add a 3/8" bead to the apron. I use an antique beading plane. If you are more into power tools you can use a router, but the plane is faster and safer! Start at one end. It is recommended that you start at the far end and work back. Repeat until the plane stops picking up a shaving. Continue on the bottom outside edges of the four aprons.

To add a round to the top of the stretcher I use a "hollow" plane, which makes a rounded edge.

The finished bead...

Use the reference marks to find the top of the stretchers. Make a pencil mark to note the depth of the curved surface on both sides.

and stretcher details. Now we are ready for gluing the ends.

Plane the top edges of the stretchers.

If there is a checking problem, which often happens in thick pieces of wood, fill it with a low viscosity glue…

and sand the surface.

I usually apply two coats of glue. First apply wood glue in the mortise…

wipe away the excess with wood chips

The result. Since this is going to be painted, this fix should be completely invisible.

and spread around with a stick or brush to create a thin, even coat. Take care in the apron blocks not to get glue in the other side of the joint. Avoid globs of glue at the bottom of the joints.

After all the joints have a first coat and it has had a few minutes to set up, go back and apply a second thin coat. The first coat acts as a sealer, giving the second coat better adhesion.

Assemble the ends, one leg...

Then the other.

Clamp the piece at the center of the tenon in line with the apron. Add spacer blocks to avoid marring the finished surface.

Clamp at the stretcher as well and put the pieces aside to dry.

When the ends are dry, glue up the front and back aprons and center stretcher in using the same techniques as you did on the ends. Carefully adjust all the joints.

Then clamp at the center of the aprons and at the center stretcher.

While the glue is setting it is a good time to put the first coat of finish on the top. I use a thinned varnish-stain mix that is mostly oil. It evens the color, penetrates the surface to condition the wood, and seals it for the next coat.

When everything is done and the glue is dried it is time to cut off the excess at the top of the leg. Carry the shoulder line to the edge with square…

and continue it around to the outside surfaces.

Cut off the line excess with a back saw.

We can now prepare for the ledger boards. Put the tabletop in place. Measure around the edges to center it on the base. When it is centered mark the outside corners of the legs on the underside of the tabletop.

Turn the top over and double check measurements to be sure the marks are correct.

This is the last good opportunity to clean up the base of the table. I look for glue spots, saw marks, and blemishes I may have missed earlier, and soften the sharp corners.

The ledger board is 1" thick and 4" wide. The length is determined by measuring 3" in from the edge of the tabletop. I want as much width as possible for strength, without interfering with people sitting at the table. Cut the board to length. The ledger board will help the top to stay flat.

Beginning about 1/8" from the edge, draw a cove down to the center at the 2" mark.

Mark the centerline of the end of the board, lengthwise.

Scribe the lines. These marks will be used as guides in designing the end of the ledger board.

Along that centerline, note the width of the board (4") and half the width (2").

Move in about 1/8" along the centerline and a draw a bead that will end up 1/8" from the other edge at the 4" mark.

Cut one end and use it as a pattern for the other ends.

The result. This is another place where you can be creative, arriving at a design that is pleasing to you.

Use a file and sandpaper to smooth the cut.

Mark out the position for the five screws that will hold the ledger to the top. They should be evenly space and allow enough space for a pin that will go through the ledger board and into the end apron.

Decide on the screw size and the countersink. With a 1" thick tabletop we want 3/4" of screw going into it. Using a 3" screw that will leave us a 1-3/4" countersink. Mark the depth of the countersink. Drill the countersink first. I use a 1/2" Forstner bit for the countersink. Drill from the other side with a bit large enough to accommodate the screw.

In order to allow for expansion of the tabletop it is necessary to slope the bottom end of the screw hole. With a hand drill, simply insert the bit in the hole and angle it one way…

then the other along the centerline of the ledger edge.

Line-up the ledger board about 1/8" outside of the line of the base you drew earlier. Be sure it is centered from side to side.

Screw the ledger board in place.

Clamp in place.

Use a 3/4" bit to drill the hole for the peg. Drill two holes in each ledger board. The holes are 7" in from the outside of the leg, or about 1/4 of the distant. They are two inches down from the bottom of the tabletop. The holes go completely through the ledger board and the apron. A piece of scrap between the ledger board and the apron will reduce the chances of chipping and splitting.

Turn the top over and position it correctly.

Use 2-1/2" x 2-1/2" stock to turn the pins. The knob will be two inches high and the stem will be 4-1/2" for a total of 6-1/2". An easy way to find center when it is not critical is to use your finger as a depth gauge and mark a square. Cross the center of the resulting square to find center.

Set your dividers to 4-1/2" and mark from each end. I am able to turn two pins from this blank.

With a parting tool reduce the stem to size just below the knob.

The pin stem is 3/4" in diameter. The knob is roughly 2". Reduce the stock to the diameter of the knob.

With a gouge, round the rest of the stem until it nears the proper diameter.

With calipers mark along the stem section for a 3/4" diameter. Clean up the stem with a skew or gouge to ensure uniformity along its length.

With a parting tool make a deep cut between the two knobs. Then begin to shape the knob to your liking, working back toward the center. Do one side first.

When you get the shape you like transfer the size to the other side and repeat.

Sand...

With a skew add some decorative rings to the knob.

and part with the skew.

Before painting the base, clean up any rough spots from the final cuttings and drillings.

I use a dry cassein paint (milk paint) mixed in water. The undercoat for the table base is barn red. You can adjust the opacity as you mix it, from the consistency of stain to an opaque consistency, which is what I use. There are no great secrets to applying the paint, except that you need complete coverage.

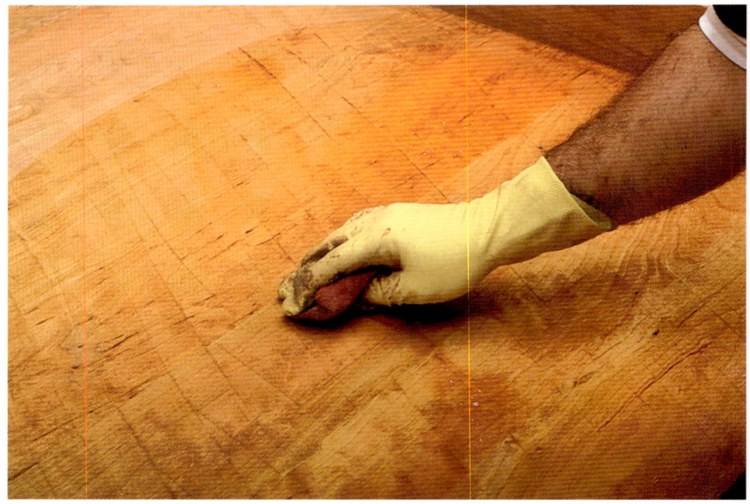

As a second coat for the tabletop I use a stronger protective varnish-oil finish. Starting with the bottom I apply a liberal coat.

After the first coat has dried I use a different color for the second coat. In this case it is black.

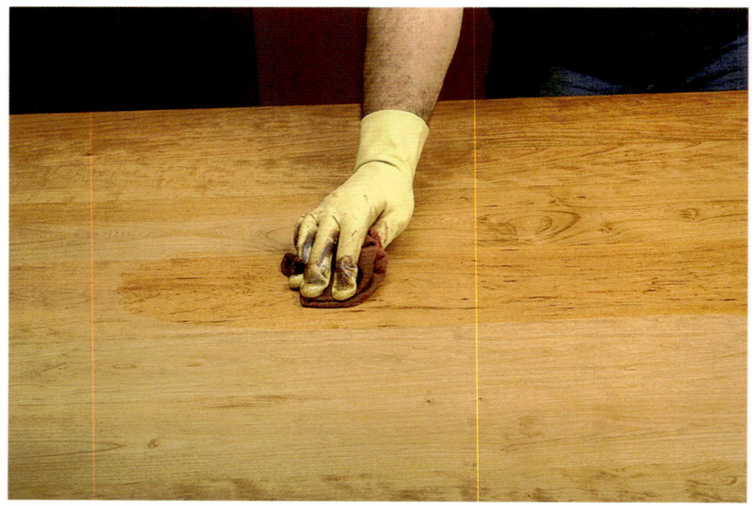

Continue with the top. Depending on the viscosity of the finish, a second or third coat may be required. Initial application can be done in any direction, followed by a light brushing in the direction of the grain.

Finally "tip" the finish with a China bristle chisel tip brush.

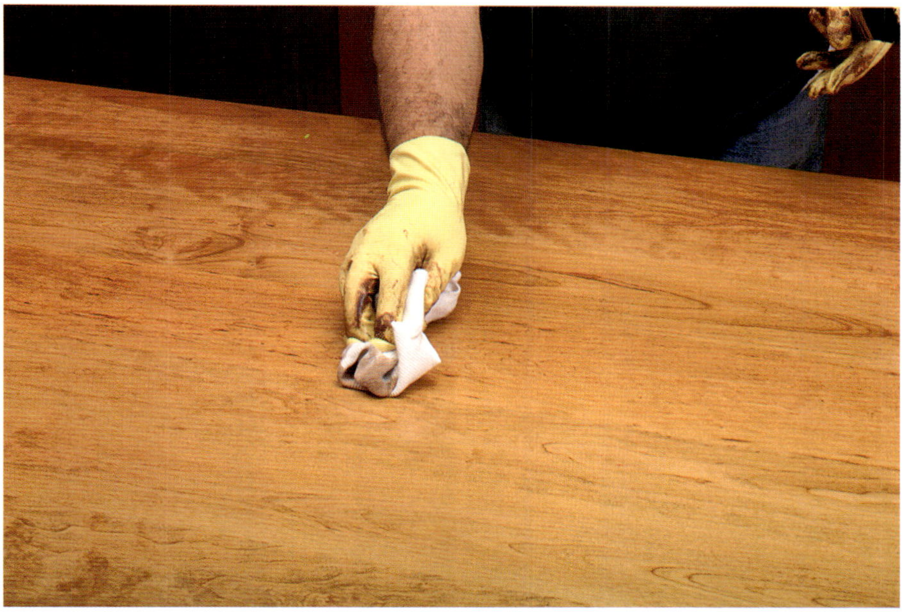

Alternatively you can use a lint free rag.

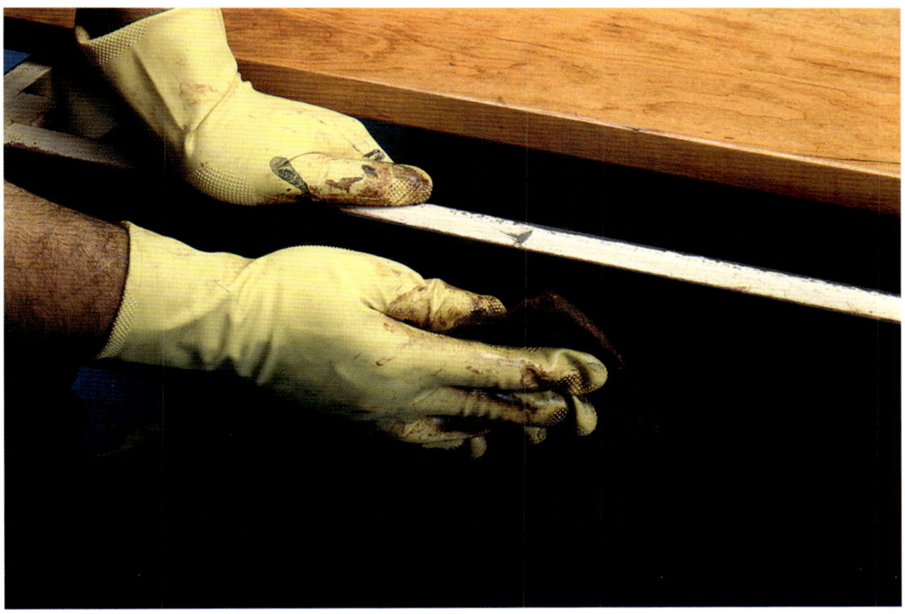

With the base paint dry, rub the surface down with an abrasive pad or steel wool. Steel wool will yield a fine sheen worth working towards before the finish.0

Apply finish on the base.

Gallery of Tavern Tables and Other Furniture